W9-AWT-207

A Very Young Musician

Written and Photographed by
Jill Krementz

NEW YORK MILLS
PUBLIC LIBRARY
NEW YORK MILLS, NY 13417

SIMON AND SCHUSTER BOOKS FOR YOUNG READERS
Published by Simon & Schuster Inc.
New York · London · Toronto · Sydney · Tokyo · Singapore

ALSO BY JILL KREMENTZ

All photographs by Jill Krementz except for
page 37 top by Wayne Brill; page 38 courtesy of
IMG Artists; and page 48 by Lars Klove.

SIMON AND SCHUSTER BOOKS FOR YOUNG READERS
Simon & Schuster Building, Rockefeller Center
1230 Avenue of the Americas, New York, New York 10020

Copyright © 1991 by Jill Krementz

All rights reserved including the right of reproduction in whole or in part in any form.
SIMON AND SCHUSTER BOOKS FOR YOUNG READERS is a trademark of Simon & Schuster Inc.
Manufactured in the United States of America

10 9 8 7 6 5 4 3 2 1

Library of Congress Cataloging-in-Publication Data
Krementz, Jill. A very young musician / written and photographed by Jill Krementz.
Summary: Text and photographs feature a boy who is learning to play the trumpet.
1. Trumpet players—Juvenile literature.   2. Music—Instruction and study—
Juvenile literature.   [1. Trumpet players.]   I. Title.   ML3928.K73 1991
788.9′2193—dc-20   90-10017   CIP   AC   MN
ISBN 0-671-72687-0

This book is dedicated to
Mary Ellin & Marvin Barrett,
with love

I love to play the trumpet. I love music. I don't know if I want to be a professional trumpet player when I grow up. All I know for sure is that I'd like to be a good musician. My name is Josh Broder and I'm ten years old.

I live in Portland, Maine, with my parents and my older brother, Yank. He's eighteen, and started out playing piano until he switched to the saxophone. He's studying composition and jazz performance at The New England Conservatory of Music. He's already decided to be a professional musician.

The first wind instrument I ever played was the shofar, which is a hollowed-out ram's horn. I heard my brother play it, so I just picked it up one day and gave it a try. I was only eight years old, but horn playing seemed to come naturally to me. My mom and dad encouraged me to try playing the trumpet. It was hard at first, but I stuck with it and pretty soon I was enjoying it. My brother was a big influence, too. He taught me a lot, and we started jamming together—me on the trumpet and Yank on the saxophone. That was the most fun of all.

I still play the shofar. My dad is president of the Jewish Home for the Aged, so I go there and play on the High Holidays. Sam and Ida tell me that it cheers them up. That makes me feel good, too.

I go to the Waynflete School and I'm in the fifth grade. My teacher's name is Mrs. Lightbody and my best friend is Matt Marston. My favorite subjects are art and science. My best sport is gymnastics. When I go back and forth to school, I usually carry my trumpet along with my school books.

Quite a few of my friends play musical instruments; and this year I was invited to join the jazz band, which is made up of all eighth graders. There are sixteen people in our ensemble. The instructor, Ray Morrow, starts each class by passing the trash can around so we can throw out our gum. Then he says, "No food, no candy, and no talking." He's a tenor saxophonist, and he taught my brother how to play when Yank was in high school. The jazz band rehearses a couple of times a week. Being a part of this older group has really built my confidence—and they've taught me a lot.

Mark Fenderson is my trumpet teacher and I have a lesson once a week at the music studio. I take an hour of private instruction and a half hour of music theory, which is done on a computer. In my practice sessions we work on the fundamentals of trumpet playing and musicianship. Mark teaches me things that are specific to my trumpet playing; but he goes beyond that and covers general musical concepts such as rhythm, intonation, and style.

Mark has a three-level reminder system to help me remember what he's told me. The first step is a gentle tap on the head with a music book. If the book doesn't work, he says he'll move to heavier objects—a tennis racket or a two-by-four. The third and by far the most effective reminder is to strangle me.

Mark makes me laugh and that's important. The main thing is to focus on what I'm doing without a lot of tension. A good musician should enjoy what he or she is doing. It's all process, not product. When you sit down to play, you're not supposed to worry about how it's going to sound to other people. You just concentrate on playing your best; and if you make a mistake, you keep on going.

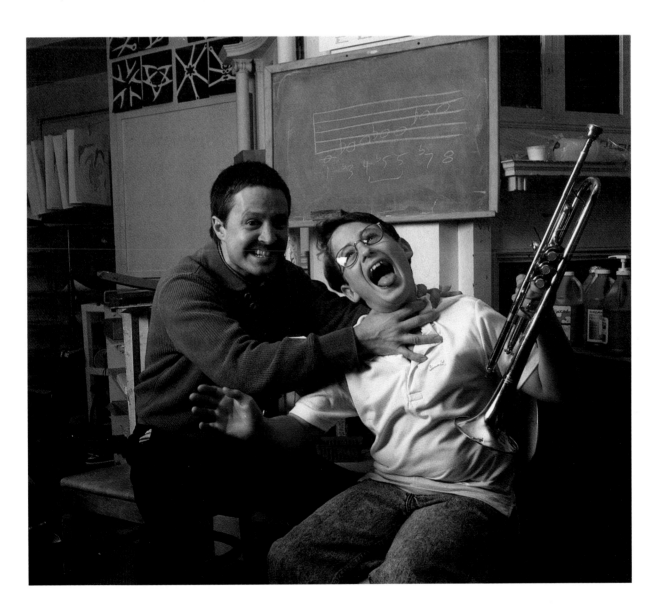

When my trumpet needs to be repaired, I take it to the Eastern Musical Supply Company in Portland. John Cullen usually works on my horn. If I'm not in a big rush, I leave it overnight; but if it's a minor problem and he's not too busy, he'll fix it while I wait. He puts my instrument on a trumpet mandrel, which allows him to take an overall look—to check and see which valves and slides are moving freely. He also checks the valve alignment so that the portholes of the valves line up with the slides to get the proper intonation of the horn.

I also buy sheet music at Eastern Music. My teacher gives me most of my practice sheets, but sometimes my mom and I like to pick out solo or duet pieces for me to practice on my own. I play orchestral pieces and chamber music, too. Some of the world's greatest composers have written music for the trumpet, and in a symphony orchestra the trumpets really shine. The parts are difficult but beautiful. It's important to study all kinds of music if you want to be a good musician, and especially if, like me, you want to write music of your own.

I try to practice every night for forty minutes. If I'm working on something new, I'll study my score ahead of time. It's crucial to be able to read new music accurately.

Early in the morning, before school and on weekends, I practice with the Deering High School Marching Band. It was a big honor to be asked to join the band and to play with people who are older and have more experience than I do.

This year I marched with the band in the Veteran's Day parade. It's hard to march and play at the same time. The music clips onto a lyre attached to the slide of my horn. It jiggles up and down as I high-step, so it's hard to read. And the mouthpiece is another problem! When I'm marching, my trumpet is moving, so it's hard to keep the mouthpiece on my lips. Besides that, it was freezing!

Lots of people came to watch, including my family. After the parade, I met a real veteran. He told me he had been a marine and fought in Vietnam for two years.

For the past two summers I've gone to a sleep-away camp called Interlochen. "Interlochen" means "between the lakes," and it's in the woods of Michigan. There are over thirteen hundred campers from all around the world who come here to study art, music, drama, and dance—and to have fun.

The camp lasts for eight weeks, and we all sleep on bunks in wooden cabins. The campers are separated by age into divisions—Junior, Intermediate, and High School. This year I was elected to represent my group—Junior Boys—in the Senate, which is our camp government. It's like a student council. I couldn't wait to go to camp again this summer because I knew I was going to have a great time and make some new friends.

Each morning, after breakfast and roll call, I check the blackboard to see if there are any special events I should know about.

Then it's off to band practice, which is always my first class of the day. Our conductor's name is Mrs. Pinckney.

It's the conductor's job to make the group perform together at the correct tempo and with the proper expression. Some conductors use their hands and others use a baton. Mrs. Pinckney uses both.

A band is made up of brass, woodwind, and percussion instruments. When there are string instruments, it's an orchestra.

You learn a lot about the other instruments when you play in a band. The woodwind section includes clarinets, bass clarinets, oboes, saxophones, flutes, piccolos, English horns, bassoons, and double bassoons. They're called "woodwinds" because many of these instruments used to be made of wood. Now some of them are made of metal, but they still have mouthpieces with wooden reeds, which you blow into to make the sound.

The saxophone is made of brass, and it combines a lot of the features of the clarinet and the oboe. Technically, it's a woodwind because its mouthpiece has a wooden reed; but since it was never made out of wood, it's sort of in a class by itself. It was invented in 1840 by a Belgian instrument maker named Adolphe Sax.

The only woodwind that doesn't use a reed is the flute. It's one of the oldest instruments—in ancient times, it was made out of clay. Flutes and recorders are part of the same family; but flutes have mouthpieces on the side, and recorders are played from the end.

The percussion instruments include the various kinds of drums—like the snare drum, the timpani, and the big bass drum—and lots of other things like triangles, castanets, cymbals, and gongs. A cymbal on a stand is called a hi-hat. In most compositions the percussion instruments aren't played much of the time, but it still takes plenty of skill to do it right. Everyone knows if you make a mistake!

The timpani are called kettledrums because that's what they are—big "kettles" of copper or brass with a skin stretched over the open top, or "head." The player uses padded drumsticks and can make a lot of different sounds, from just a whisper to a big roar that sounds like thunder.

The brass section sits in the back of the band because it's the loudest. It includes the trumpet, trombone, French horn, and tuba. This year there were three trumpet players in the band—Dorie, Louis, and me.

The French horn originated in France as a hunting horn and is very difficult to play. French horn players always seem to put one of their hands inside the instrument bell, and this is called "stopping." The effect is a more muffled tone that sounds smoother and more velvety.

When we're learning a new piece, Mrs. Pinckney rehearses each section separately until we get it right. Then when we all play together, it's like a miracle—all these different people playing different instruments to make music. We probably play our best when we give concerts. There's a lot of pressure when you're playing for an audience and you can't hear what the band sounds like. But when you hear the applause at the end, it's one of the greatest feelings I know.

Once a week, after lunch, I have a private lesson with Craig Davis. On the days I don't have lessons, I practice.

It's very important to keep my instrument clean. It's dark inside the trumpet, and the dampness from my breath makes it easy for mold to grow there. I wash my trumpet out about once a month; and every day that I play, I begin by removing the valves and oiling them one at a time. Then I clean and oil the main tuning slide and adjust it so I'll be in tune when I play with other people.

There are many different techniques that go into playing the trumpet. Sometimes Craig and I start our lesson with mouthpiece buzzing. It's called "buzzing" because that's what it sounds like when you vibrate your lips against the mouthpiece. It takes a little more endurance to get a good buzz on the mouthpiece when it's not attached to the trumpet. That's because the trumpet is like a loudspeaker, and it amplifies the sound.

Mouthpiece buzzing makes your lips stronger. This helps develop "embouchure," which means how you shape your lips and tongue when you blow into the mouthpiece. Most jazz musicians refer to embouchure as "chops."

Craig shows me how to finger the valves that control the pitches of the trumpet. The valves are on top, and I move them with fingers that are held firm. There are seven possible fingering combinations on the trumpet. That means you can play a lot of different notes. But you also have to think about the sound and the speed of each note. You have to coordinate how you blow into the mouthpiece and how you finger the valves to get just the right effect.

Craig tells me how important it is to fill up my horn. After I've warmed up, he says, "Now we're going to see how long you can tongue one note." He reminds me to keep the air moving through my instrument as I play lip slurs—that's when you go from one note to another note without pressing any valves. Lip slurs are exercises that build endurance, range, and lip flexibility, and develop breath support.

Trumpet players are all good kissers. At least that's what my girlfriends say.

I don't spend the whole day practicing or playing. In the afternoons, I take a nature course called Environmental Exploration. We go river wading, watch movies, and sometimes find wonderful Indian arrowheads and old pieces of pottery. Our camp is on Duck Lake, so we also do a lot of swimming.

At the end of the day, I usually jam with my friends Jeff and Louis. We play jazz to a background tape of percussion, bass, and piano. Jamming is a lot of fun, and quite a bit different from playing in a band or an orchestra. You don't always have to stick to the notes. You can improvise and express yourself by playing the music in different ways. You're playing together as a group, but you always have a chance to show what you can really do. Jeff, Louis, and I get along great; and I figure we'll probably be friends for the rest of our lives.

At Interlochen, the students who are studying dance put on ballet recitals and the drama students put on plays. The artists exhibit their crafts and paintings, and sometimes they even exhibit themselves. We all have a chance to see these performances. We also have the opportunity to show off what we've learned. For me, that's one of the things that makes camp so much fun.

All summer long we have famous performers who hold master classes for the students and who perform in the evenings. This year Itzhak Perlman and Billy Taylor—two of my favorites—were guest artists. Itzhak Perlman played a violin concerto with the camp's World Youth Symphony Orchestra. Billy Taylor played piano with his trio.

When I got home from camp, my mom and dad took me to a Wynton Marsalis concert on Long Island to celebrate my eleventh birthday. He's one of my favorite musicians so this was a special treat. The concert was at a club called Wings. Since I usually set up the sound system for my brother's performances, I knew Wynton would probably be there an hour or two before the concert for a sound check. So I went early; hoping to meet him. Was I ever lucky! He did arrive early, and since I was the only one there, besides the waiters, I sat and watched while he and the rest of his ensemble rehearsed.

Wynton Marsalis is not only a great trumpet player, he's also a great musician. He can play anything from classical concertos to modern jazz. He asked me if I had brought along my horn. I had, and he asked me to play for him. I was scared to death, but I played my long tones and some slur exercises.

Then he played his trumpet. He put my hand on his windpipe so he could demonstrate deep breathing—using a lot of air when you're playing—which is essential to trumpet playing. He told me how important it is to practice, to relax when I play, and to be humble. He said I should work on my scales; make every exercise musical; practice every day; and when I'm practicing to concentrate on every detail—to always know the reason why I'm practicing something. If I do all these things, he said, I'll be really good.

Wynton started playing when he was six and practicing seriously when he was twelve. His brother, Branford, is a great musician, too. Besides playing tenor saxophone, Branford has acted in quite a few movies. They both learned a lot from their father, who is head of the jazz department at the University of New Orleans.

At the end of the lesson, Wynton told me that I should always help other musicians and practice every day—he said that it shows in your tone.

While we waited for his concert to begin, I told my mom and dad that I would remember this birthday until I was a hundred years old.

The concert was wonderful! Wynton and the ensemble played "The New Orleans Function," which is a favorite of mine. It's one of the pieces from his album called "Majesty of the Blues." Between each set, he talked to the audience about the growth and history of jazz.

It's hard to believe that he's only twenty-seven years old. He's won eight Grammies, and he's the only musician who has ever won a Grammy for both jazz and classical music in the same year.

During the concert, I tried to imagine what it would be like if that was me up there. Wynton made it look so easy, but I know that hours and hours of practice go into every piece. I could tell that he loves music and loves to play for people.

Meeting Wynton Marsalis and getting to play for him was one of the most exciting things that ever happened to me. I still haven't decided if I want to be a full-time trumpet player when I grow up. I know I have a lot to learn. For now, I just want to be a better musician. But if I do stay with serious playing, I hope I'll always be as nice to young musicians as Wynton was to me.

Josh and Jill

JILL KREMENTZ works as a journalist, photographer, and portraitist. Her pictures can be seen regularly in *The New York Times, Los Angeles Times, New York* Magazine, *Time, Newsweek,* and many other major periodicals. She has written and photographed more than two dozen books for young readers and adults, including *A Very Young Skier, A Very Young Dancer, A Very Young Rider, A Very Young Gymnast, A Very Young Circus Flyer, A Very Young Skater, The Fun of Cooking, A Visit to Washington, D.C.,* and the "How It Feels" series dealing with the death of a parent, adoption, divorce and chronic illness.

Ms. Krementz received the 1984 *Washington Post*/Children's Book Guild Nonfiction Award for "creatively produced books, works that make a difference." She lives in New York City with her husband and young daughter.